# VIRGO

*This Book Belongs To*

Elmira R.

# VIRGO

*The Sign of the Virgin*
*August 24 – September 23*

By Teresa Celsi
and Michael Yawney

*Ariel Books*

*Andrews and McMeel*
*Kansas City*

## VIRGO

ISBN: 0–8362–3080–9
Library of Congress Catalog Card Number: 93-73359

# Contents

Astrology—An Introduction     *7*

The Sign of the Virgin     *12*

Character and Personality     *14*

Signs and Symbols     *18*

Health and Fitness     *20*

Home and Family     *22*

Careers and Goals     *24*

Pastimes and Play     *26*

Love Among the Signs     *28*

Virgo with Aries     *32*

Virgo with Taurus     *36*

Virgo with Gemini 40

Virgo with Cancer 44

Virgo with Leo 48

Virgo with Virgo 52

Virgo with Libra 56

Virgo with Scorpio 60

Virgo with Sagittarius 64

Virgo with Capricorn 68

Virgo with Aquarius 72

Virgo with Pisces 76

# Astrology

## An Introduction

**E**arly in our history, as human-kind changed from hunter-gatherers to farmers, they left the forests and moved to the plains, where they could raise plants and live-stock. While they guarded their animals at night, the herders gazed up at the sky. They watched the stars circle Earth, counted the days between moons, and perceived an order in the universe.

Astrology was born as a way of finding a meaningful relationship between the movements of the heavens and the events on Earth. Astrologers believe that the celestial dance of planets affects our personalities and destinies. In order to better understand these forces, an astrologer creates a chart, which is like a snapshot of the heavens at the time of your birth. Each planet—Mercury, Venus, Mars, Jupiter, Saturn, Uranus, Neptune, and Pluto—has influence on you. So does the place of your birth.

The most important element in a chart is your sun sign, commonly known as your astrological sign. There are twelve signs of the zodiac, a belt of sky encircling Earth that is divided into twelve zones. Whichever zone the sun was in at your time of birth determines your sun sign. Your sun sign influences conscious behavior. Your moon sign influences unconscious behavior. (This book deals only with sun signs. To find your moon sign, you must look in a reference book or consult an astrologer.)

Each sign is categorized under one of the four elements: *fire*, *earth*, *air*, or *water*. Fire signs (Aries, Leo, and Sagittarius) are creative and somewhat self-centered. Earth signs (Taurus, Virgo, and Capricorn) are steady and desire material things. Air signs (Gemini, Libra, and Aquarius) are clever and intellectual.

Water signs (Cancer, Scorpio, and Pisces) are emotional and empathetic.

Each sign has one of three qualities—*cardinal*, *fixed*, or *mutable*—which shows how it operates. Cardinal signs (Aries, Cancer, Libra, and Capricorn) use their energy to lead in a direct, forceful way. Fixed signs (Taurus, Leo, Scorpio, and Aquarius) harness energy and use it to organize and consolidate. Mutable signs (Gemini, Virgo, Sagittarius, and Pisces) use energy to transform and change.

Every sign has a different combination of an element and a quality. When the positions of all the twelve planets are added to a chart, you can begin to appreciate the complexity of each individ-

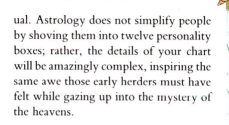

ual. Astrology does not simplify people by shoving them into twelve personality boxes; rather, the details of your chart will be amazingly complex, inspiring the same awe those early herders must have felt while gazing up into the mystery of the heavens.

# The Sign of the Virgin

Like the Virgin, under whose sign they are born, Virgos are the embodiment of purity, devotion, and service. This sign is associated with fertility goddesses, in particular Demeter, the Greek goddess of the harvest who gave earth's bounty to the world. Like Demeter's, Virgo's essential nature is to enrich humankind selflessly.

In mythology and religion, the virgin

is often associated with the birth of gods and others whose offspring have significance for humankind. The Virgin Mary, for example, gave birth to Jesus, the Christian savior who took the sins of the world upon himself.

Virgo is ruled by Mercury, the planet revolving closest to the sun. The son of Jupiter, king of the gods, Mercury was the Roman messenger of the gods. This swift and precocious young deity gathered information and spread it far and wide. And so the planet, like the messenger, represents the power to communicate of those born under the sign of Virgo.

## Character and Personality

**B**eing born under the sign of the Virgin has nothing to do with being a virgin in a literal sense. Virgo might give the impression of being uptight or repressed, but this is a facade. What you are actually seeing is self-control. This sun sign excels in mastering its emotions and in all other aspects of life.

Virgo is a mutable earth sign. Mutability is linked with change and transformation, while the element of earth grounds Virgo firmly in reality. Some mutable signs have trouble focusing and can feel overwhelmed by the complexity of their thoughts or emotions. But the element of earth allows Virgo to build its dream castles on a firm, practical foundation.

The Virgin is tireless in analyzing anything and everything. This sign is a master at arranging and organizing its world in order to find not just the best but the perfect solution.

Improvement is the guiding force behind Virgo. For this sun sign, the world is a huge machine whose parts are to be observed and analyzed so its operation can be perfected. Virgo seems always to be in a battle between order and chaos.

You can be sure that after thorough examination of any issue, Virgo will not be shy about voicing its suggestions for improvement. Others may interpret these as unnecessary or even hostile criticisms, but Virgo is motivated by honesty, not hostility. For the Virgin, it's simply a matter of making things better.

Virgo's zeal is not without fault. The Virgin can be fussy and narrow-minded, complaining about the smallest things. And it is difficult for Virgo to admit he or she is wrong. Yet this sign is invariably harder on itself than it is on others.

Virgo will always speak plainly and directly, paying precise attention to details. Its ruling planet, Mercury, has blessed this sign with the capacity for simplicity and clarity in expression and communication.

Even while striving for perfection, Virgo does not expend energy foolishly. Prudent and practical, this sign has an almost unlimited capacity for work and service to others. Devotion and loyalty are also strengths of this sun sign. Traits like these allow others to forgive Virgo's critical (and sometimes unyielding) nature.

# Signs and Symbols

E ach sign in the zodiac is ruled by a different planet. Virgo is ruled by Mercury, named after the Roman messenger of the gods.

Virgo is symbolized by the Virgin, which figures in ancient mythology as a symbol of fertility and earth. Animals associated with Virgo are cats, small dogs, and domestic fowl.

The sixth sign of the zodiac, Virgo

combines the element of earth (sensuality) with the mutable quality of transforming energy. This sign is essentially a scientist—a practical and analytical thinker. Virgos are intelligent, critical, and sometimes anxious.

Virgo is linked with Wednesday and rules the stomach and intestines. Its lucky number is seven. Brown, navy blue, violet, white, and gray are Virgo's colors; nickel and mercury are its metals; and sapphire is its gemstone.

Flowers linked with Virgo are the buttercup and forget-me-not. Its foods are chicken, endive, and grains, such as oats and millet.

# Health and Fitness

oderation is this sign's hallmark. While not especially fond of strenuous exercise, Virgos engage in regular workouts and watch their diets carefully, avoiding foods that disagree with them. This sign is not likely to overindulge.

Health is a major concern for those born under this sun sign, but not because they are sickly. On the contrary, Virgos are quite healthy. They can, however, literally worry themselves into illness.

Virgo rules the intestinal system. Those born under this sign tend to suffer from digestive or nervous disorders. Often these kinds of illnesses are the result of emotional upsets brought about by the Virgin's tendency to keep feelings bottled up. They can also suffer from lack of rest.

Fortunately for Virgos, they are quite resilient. Once ill, they assess their predicament and take the appropriate steps to get better, usually springing back quickly.

# Home and Family

The minute you walk into a Virgo home, you'll know it. All the clocks will be set to precisely the right time. The furniture will look as if it were brand new. And the floors will be clean enough to eat from. Of course you won't have to because the table already will be set—with matching dishes, silver, glassware, and linen. Virgos are the zodiac's perfectionists, and it is reflected in their homes.

Those born under this sun sign are fond of children—theirs and other people's. Their children will be organized and well behaved; no Virgo parent would accept any less from its child. This sign sometimes demands much from its own offspring, but to other people's children, it can be an excellent chum.

Virgo children need encouragement far more than criticism. When they make mistakes, they are harder on themselves than their parents are. They tend to develop routines and stick to them. They should be encouraged to add variety to their play and to be less judgmental of their capabilities.

# Careers and Goals

The employer who hires a Virgo will be rewarded with a precise, meticulous, and ambitious worker. The Virgin excels in any job where attention to detail is of prime importance. Virgo's employer, however, should be prepared to listen to suggestions for improvements—and possibly some criticism of its operations.

This sign's health concerns can sometimes interfere with work. If they are not feeling well, Virgos will stay home, even if a project is at a critical stage. To Virgo, this is responsible behavior: After all, it is better to maintain one's health than to wreck it by overworking.

Virgo's ruling planet, Mercury, often nudges those born under this sign into areas of communication, such as publishing, radio or television, acting, or politics. Their gift for precision makes Virgos excellent dietitians, accountants, financiers, or attorneys. Because of their drive to serve others, Virgos are also attracted to the health-care professions.

## Pastimes and Play

V irgo prefers solitary pursuits to group activities. When it comes to sports, the Virgin is more likely to walk, ride a bicycle, or play golf than to participate in a volleyball game.

The most likely place to find the Virgin is at a gym, working out on an exercise machine. The Virgin engages in physical activities for the health benefits more than for fun, since exercise is a means to an end.

Virgos love to read, another solitary pastime. They enjoy nonfiction and art or political criticism as much or more than fiction. The Virgo home will probably have a reading area with specially designed lighting to prevent eyestrain.

Virgos also enjoy parties, but they prefer them to be small affairs with good friends. Attending movies and plays gives the Virgin pleasure, but they are very selective in what they choose to see. Virgo won't go out just to be doing something. It prefers entertainment that is intellectually and visually stimulating.

# Love Among the Signs

**W**hat is attraction? What is love? Throughout the centuries, science has tried and failed to come up with a satisfying explanation for the mysterious connection between two people.

For the astrologer, the answer is clear. The position of the planets at the time of your birth creates a pattern that influences you throughout your lifetime.

When your pattern meets another person's, the two of you might clash or harmonize.

Why this mysterious connection occurs can be explored only by completing charts for both individuals. But even if the chemistry is there, will it be a happy relationship? Will it last? No one can tell for certain.

Every relationship requires give-and-take, and an awareness of the sun sign relationships can help with this process. The sun sign influences conscious behavior. Does your lover catalog the items in the medicine cabinet? Chances are you have a Virgo on your hands. Do you like to spend your weekends running while your lover wants to play Scrabble? This could be an Aries-Gemini combination.

To discover more about your relationship, find out your lover's sun sign and look under the appropriate combination. You may learn things you had never even suspected.

## Virgo with Aries

*(March 21– April 20)*

A ries has an audacity that takes Virgo's breath away. Virgo thinks the Ram is fearless, risking failure or personal injury with reckless abandon. Virgo is far too cautious to rush headlong into life the way Aries does.

The truth is, Aries displays great physical courage because it is essentially an overgrown child, and children are often brave because they don't yet know the world can be a dangerous place. To Virgo, Aries' childish nature is not becoming. The Virgin wants the Ram to grow up and act like an adult.

Another problem this pair faces springs from a common trait: Both freely express their critical natures. Virgo, however, offers criticism only after much reflection and sincerely wants to be helpful. On the other hand, Aries' criticisms stem from its inability to hold anything back. Motivated by a fierce desire to win, the self-centered Ram will spout off without consideration for the other person or the situation.

Aries' thoughtless outbursts offend Virgo's sense of moderation and decorum. As for Aries, any criticism aimed at it, no matter how carefully considered, can bring on a tantrum. But the Ram won't stay mad for long. In a few minutes, the offending remark will be forgotten. Unfortunately, any lesson it might have learned from the criticism is often forgotten as well.

Conflict between these partners may at first be offset by romance. Aries is a passionate, generous lover, and Virgo possesses hidden fires. But the Ram may lack the patience to stoke the smoldering flames and may eventually find Virgo a bit dull. The Virgin, on the other hand, may be offended by the Ram's "me-first" attitude.

If used in the right way, these signs' opposing qualities could help each other in personal and business matters. Fire sign Aries is a creative visionary who always sees the big picture. It can be shaky on the details, however, and it's here that Virgo's admirable attention to the fine points will be appreciated.

Virgo can help Aries fulfill some of its wild dreams by seeing to the actual details. The Ram can help channel the Virgin's talent for meticulous precision into a firm, purposeful direction. At the least, this relationship will teach these two a great deal about patience.

## Virgo with Taurus

### (April 21–May 21)

**V**irgo cares most for order. Taurus cares most for comfort. Not a good mix, one would think. Yet this can be one of the most harmonious pairings of the zodiac.

As earth signs who have many qualities in common, Virgo and Taurus are exceptionally tolerant of what others would deem their shortcomings. Virgo may cluck over the dirty dishes but will forgive Taurus, since the Bull doesn't insist on rearranging Virgo's carefully organized cupboards. Virgo admires the Bull's ability to accomplish difficult tasks and to keep a regular schedule, arriving home at the same time every day.

Others may chafe at Virgo's criticism, but Taurus is blessed with almost inexhaustible patience. The Bull not only listens to Virgo's suggestions but frequently carries them out.

Although Taurus basks in Virgo's devotion, the Bull can be a jealous partner. But Taurus need not worry about Virgo. The Virgin is among the most devoted and faithful signs of the zodiac.

Taurus is a slow, steady, and sensual

lover—exactly what Virgo wants in a mate. Though there may not be any pyrotechnics in the bedroom, these two signs, both loving and affectionate, can create enough passion to keep both of them satisfied for a lifetime.

On all the important domestic matters—home, family, money—Virgo and Taurus will agree. Virgo is more interested in the house itself—both inside and out. Taurus has a deep need to work the soil, even if it's just a few houseplants or a window box full of sweet peas and geraniums. For Virgo, the newer the house or apartment the better—to the fastidious Virgin, new means less dirt and grime.

The children of these two can count on devoted parents and a stable home environment. When these children reach adolescence, however, Virgo's concerns may be expressed too critically, and Taurus may become a stubborn, rigid disciplinarian. Both will find their patience taxed when their children enter the difficult teen years.

The pairing of the Virgin and the Bull is a happy, productive, and supportive one. As the years go by, this relationship will only become more fulfilling and rewarding.

# Virgo with Gemini

## *(May 22–June 21)*

I f Virgo wants variety, there is no better way to find it than in a Gemini. This mutable air sign, whose symbol is the Twins, has the ability to change its personality at will. Life with Gemini will never be dull.

It might be a little lonely, however. Gemini needs constant mental stimulation and seeks it out in social activities and travel. Virgo enjoys the company of others but doesn't like to socialize as frequently as Gemini does. Eventually, the Virgin will want to settle down. Though the Twins need the sort of stable environment that Virgo can provide, this sign is essentially an explorer and will find it difficult to stay in one place for long.

While Gemini is around, however, the place will ring with laughter. These signs share Mercury, the planet that rules the mind and communication. Together, the Virgin and the Twins can amuse each other wittily for hours. These revelries, even though stimulating, will eventually frustrate Virgo, who wants to get to the heart of things and will find Gemini's tendency to skim the surface of every subject increasingly upsetting.

These two play and work well together, since both are clever, inventive, and meticulous. But that doesn't mean they should start their own business. Neither one is characterized by driving ambition. Then, too, their fussiness and worry over detail could be a bone of contention. Working for others would be a much more rewarding solution.

Some conflicts will arise in the intimate aspects of this relationship. To Gemini, lovemaking is a game that demands innovation and variety. Virgo is

willing to go along with experiments—to a point.

Any close relationship between the Virgin and the Twins is bound to be fraught with friction and conflict. These two can be close friends, enjoying each other's company and conversation. Each, though, needs more than it can get from the other. If they do enter into a partnership (personal or business), they need time away from each other to recharge their batteries and recover from the stimulation of their combined mercurial cleverness. Their time apart will make their time together more special and harmonious.

43

## Virgo with Cancer

### (June 22–July 23)

**B**oth Virgo and Cancer have a strong need to give of themselves. Virgo likes to nurse others; Cancer likes to nourish others. You might think this relationship was made in heaven.

Not exactly. Cancer is vulnerable to suggestion, especially where health is concerned. If Virgo starts fussing about Cancer's well-being, the Crab starts fretting as well. Together, they can worry a cold into pneumonia. In matters of health, the Crab is better off with someone who has a more optimistic outlook.

On the other hand, Virgo will be irritated with Cancer's food obsession. For Virgo, food is simply a means to keep the body in good working order. To Cancer, food is an expression of love. If Cancer feels low, it will indulge and urge its partner to do the same. However, when Cancer starts piling on the mashed potatoes, Virgo may lose patience and strike out painfully at the already fragile Crab.

A business relationship between these two could work. Although both are adept at business concerns, they have different areas of expertise—Cancer is especially good with money, whereas Virgo excels at improving efficiency. If they allow each other to handle their separate departments free from advice or interference, their business relationship can prosper.

In a romantic partnership, Cancer craves security and harmony. Under its protective shell, the Crab hides an extremely sensitive nature. Virgo must make sure the intimate time it spends with Cancer is special and romantic. Nothing will cause the Crab to retreat into its shell more than aloof lovemaking.

Ruled by the moon, Cancer is subject to varying temperaments. The Crab can

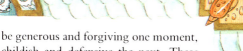

be generous and forgiving one moment, childish and defensive the next. These mood swings may be trying to Virgo, who always appears composed.

Cancer will have a difficult time understanding Virgo's need for solitude. To keep Cancer happy and secure, Virgo must be understanding and tolerant, which is not always easy for the Virgin. And Cancer will have to learn that Virgo's need for privacy doesn't mean the Virgin no longer wants to be with the Crab.

The union of these two signs can be relatively peaceful if both work toward making their partnership a blend of sympathy and reason.

## Virgo with Leo

### (July 24–August 23)

L eo, ruled by the power of the
sun, is used to overwhelming
others with the force of its personality. Charismatic and attractive, Leo
sincerely believes its charm is irresistible.
Virgo, however, regards the Lion with
a cool, appraising eye; the Virgin isn't
swayed by charisma or a good perfor-
mance but attempts to see beyond ap-
pearances to what is essential.

If there is substance to the Lion, the Virgin will begin to warm up. And if things go well, this relationship can deepen. However, if the Lion is all show, Virgo will be unimpressed. Since Leo secretly fears it lacks substance, the presence of a critical Virgo can turn Leo into a cowardly Lion.

Some of Leo's traits offend Virgo. Though the Virgin is not intimidated by the Lion's roar, it finds the Lion's bullying tactics unbearable. And Leo's tendency to act up in front of an audience also disturbs the Virgin, who hates making scenes of any kind.

Virgo will find Leo's self-centeredness hard to take. When Virgo gathers information, it is to find out more about the world; Leo wants only to find out more about itself—and it wants to hear only the good things.

Virgo's habit of pointing out faults is more than the Lion can handle. Leo needs constant reassurance that it is good, brave, smart, and loved. It can take criticism only if it is couched within compliments.

These two clash in the bedroom, too. Leo is a passionate, aggressive lover who tends to overwhelm a partner. Virgo needs tenderness and restraint more than gusto. On the other hand, Virgo's critical nature may cool the Lion's ardor considerably.

A business partnership would be a good match for these two signs. Virgo will appreciate Leo's innate charisma and leadership abilities—assets to any business. The Lion will expect Virgo to do the drudgery work, but the Virgin won't mind handling the details.

Friendship might be the best bet for this pair. Too much is at stake in a romantic relationship for these two to tolerate each other's flaws. In friendship, Virgo tends to be a big brother or sister toward Leo—tolerant, proud, and a bit condescending; Leo, knowing it will benefit from its friend's advice, will be surprisingly willing to take it—and be a loyal friend.

# Virgo with Virgo

### *(August 24–September 23)*

hen two people share the same sun sign, they tend to magnify each other's positive and negative traits. The positive traits of a Virgo include grace, courtesy, trustworthiness, discrimination, and common sense. The negative ones include timidity, crankiness, and pessimism.

Imagine two Virgos arranging and organizing a dinner party: It would be the best-managed party the guests had ever seen. Then imagine two Virgo attorneys sitting around arguing a point of law. This could go on forever since neither side is likely to admit it could be wrong. The key to this relationship is for each partner to encourage the positive qualities of the other while gently tolerating the negative aspects.

When two Virgos get together, they benefit from having the same attitudes and approaches to life. Both are practical, rather than eccentric, individualists. Money is important to them because of what it can do. It will be spent wisely on useful and tasteful objects or invested in a safe pension fund. Whatever Virgos do together, they will discuss it in detail and come up with a mutually satisfying plan.

Virgos, despite their mutuality, will fare better in separate work places. If they spend too much time working together, their analytical natures can cause friction. It is almost certain they will end up criticizing each other. With different jobs, each can lend a sympathetic ear and offer helpful suggestions to the other without feeling personally involved.

In the bedroom these two will get along well. It won't be fireworks—that's not Virgo's style—but it will be gentle, loving, responsive, and satisfying. Infidelity is rarely an issue with these two since Virgos are famous for their loyalty—in bed and out.

The goal of a Virgo–Virgo relationship should be self-fulfillment and self-mastery, not the improvement of the partner. These two signs must be careful not to let their tendency to find fault develop into constant, nagging criticism. If they're successful, this relationship will be as smooth as a well waxed floor—something they both appreciate.

## Virgo with Libra

### (September 24–October 23)

t first, Virgo and Libra seem like the perfect couple: Libra will admire the Virgin's integrity and individuality as well as Virgo's head for organization or detail; Virgo highly approves of Libra's sense of justice and envies this sign's easy social graces and overtly joyous nature. The Virgin is flattered by Libra's attentiveness, and Libra handles Virgo's demanding nature with tact and diplomacy.

However, beneath this surface compatibility lie deep differences. Libra, the sign of the Scales, cherishes balance and harmony in relationships. The relationship is more important to Libra than the individuals in it. Virgo, who values individuality above everything else, sees the partners as two separate entities and may resent it if Libra takes control and starts making decisions for both of them. The Scales just naturally assume that the two partners are in agreement about everything.

Libra is an attention-loving social butterfly whose constant activities will wear down Virgo's nerves and patience. Virgo is not comfortable making small talk—one of Libra's many social skills.

Virgo may also find Libra's sentimental streak annoying. The Scales adores flowers and lace, chocolates and candlelight. For pragmatic Virgo, this is unnecessary nonsense. The Virgin can mercilessly denigrate the flowers as wasteful, the chocolates as expensive, and the candlelight as ridiculous. Criticism like this will be devastating to Libra and squelch any further romantic gestures.

Although Virgo and Libra are not likely to run into the same problems in a business relationship, there are other dangers here. An air sign, the Scales often view life as a marvelous puzzle or game, and business is not likely to be an exception. The Virgin, however, doesn't play around; Virgo takes business seriously. Libra does not. When the going gets tough, Libra may jump ship, leaving Virgo to weather the storm alone.

Both signs hate confrontation. Still, if they are to have a lasting partnership, they must be direct, honest, and sympathetic with each other. Most important, both must be true to themselves and avoid making sacrifices they will later resent.

## Virgo with Scorpio

### *(October 24–November 22)*

S corpio, a fixed water sign whose symbol is the Scorpion, is the most quietly powerful sign in the zodiac. This sign can be so consuming that others often keep a safe distance in order to preserve their own identities. Scorpio is not for the faint of heart. Though the Virgin may appear nervous and timid, it has a strong sense of self and can safely approach the Scorpion.

These two will not be immediately

attracted to each other and may meet with their defenses up. Virgo will be all emotional detachment and critical objectivity. Scorpio, too, will be aloof, its coolness coming from a complete masking of emotions.

Once they are close, however, Virgo will discover Scorpio has a gentle nature. That cold hard shell is there to protect a vulnerable soft interior. Scorpio will discover that Virgo is not as cold as the Virgin first appeared. That critical Virgo nature, which sends Aries howling for mommy and Leo skulking back to the den, will not be a problem for Scorpio, who can see that Virgo's motivation is to improve and perfect.

This acceptance helps them work together. Both are aware of their capabilities and limits. Virgo's innate sense of self-worth keeps it from succumbing to Scorpio's sometimes outrageous demands, and Scorpio's strong self-confidence allows it to listen to Virgo's advice.

Security is important for these signs. They will save money easily and make secure investments, never gambling with their future. Their home will probably be secluded and neat, with well-chosen furnishings.

Contentions can arise in the bedroom, though. Sexually, Scorpio comes on strong and often delights in variations in lovemaking. This is an area where Virgo is likely to hold back. However, if Scorpio is loving and gentle, the Virgin might trust the Scorpion enough to be coaxed into some mutually enjoyable variety.

In fact, trust will be the real basis of their lives together, whether in love, business, or friendship. Both value commitment over everything else in a relationship. While this pairing may never be an all-consuming grand passion, it will give them great happiness. Even if the rest of the world lets them down, these two know they can always trust each other.

# Virgo with Sagittarius

## (November 23–December 21)

These two sun signs share similar missions in life. Both the Virgin and the Archer, Sagittarius's symbol, are out to redesign, improve, and, ideally, perfect the great machine called the world. The Archer, however, being more interested in what the machine does than how it works, is more likely to just point out the machine's flaws rather than actually try to fix it.

For example, should Sagittarius discover that a factory is producing harmful chemicals, the Archer will, with devastating accuracy and humor, puncture the pretensions of the factory's misleading advertising campaign. Virgo, on the other hand, will be too busy improving the efficiency of the assembly line to bother about what the factory is making.

Virgo may sacrifice the large picture for the detail, and Sagittarius may do just the reverse. This can cause problems in all areas of their relationship.

Neither the Archer nor the Virgin is overly ambitious. A business relationship would definitely not be in their best interests. As two mutable signs, they can have trouble finding direction and will not be much help to each other in practical ways. Mutable signs need the grounding of the fixed signs or the direction of the cardinal signs to be truly effective in business.

Personal relationships need direction as well—at least for Virgo. If the Virgin is going to marry or have a love affair, it wants agreed-upon terms and conditions. Sagittarius doesn't. The restless Archer wants loose arrangements and no restrictions. Trying to pin down Sagittarius is difficult. Virgo may finally have to throw up its hands and accept an uneasy compromise.

A committed sexual relationship between these partners can run into real problems: The freedom-loving Archer is likely to be less than monogamous, and Virgo is not one to put up with sexual infidelity in a mate.

The Archer and the Virgin will be in for a challenging relationship. Neither sign will be truly comfortable with the other and they are more likely to become friends than lovers. However, should these two decide to pursue a relationship, an honest assessment of their differences and how to compensate for them should be their first priority.

## Virgo with Capricorn

### (December 22–January 20)

L ike Virgo, Capricorn, whose symbol is the Goat, is an earth sign. These two view the world in much the same way. Capricorn's desire for order, structure, responsibility, and security combine beautifully with Virgo's menu for happiness.

These two do differ in one area, however—ambition. Capricorn thirsts for success and is single-minded in trying to achieve it. However, the Goat's ambition will not be a drawback for Virgo and if Virgo has trouble finding a way to apply its talents, Capricorn will provide the direction.

Because both these signs often feel that disaster lurks just around the corner, they covet security. And security to Capricorn and Virgo means money. Although they would rather save a penny than spend it, when they do shell out, you can bet that the purchase will be sturdy and practical.

Security in their relationship is also of crucial importance. If the Goat and the Virgin are together for any length of time, they will probably tie the knot. As business partners, too, their association will be lasting. Neither sign makes rash decisions, and each admires in the other those tendencies that other people sometimes find irritating, such as Virgo's criticisms, which the loyal Capricorn finds quite useful. The Virgin respects the Goat's drive and may even harbor a secret desire to be as aggressive.

In lovemaking, these two draw out in each other qualities that are usually kept hidden. The Goat, afraid of not being taken seriously by others, loosens up considerably when Virgo is around. With Virgo, who admires Capricorn, the Goat is free to be playful, even silly. Since the Goat tends to be nervous in the bedroom, Virgo's gentleness will help transform Capricorn into a more relaxed lover.

Problems could arise from Capricorn's periodic bouts of depression. The Goat's black moods can last for days or even weeks. Virgo, who is more flexible, may have difficulty understanding why Capricorn can't just snap out of it and get on with things. Being sensitive and practical, however, Virgo will learn to anticipate Capricorn's blue moods and counter them with love and reassurance.

## Virgo with Aquarius

### (January 21–February 19)

A quarius, an air sign symbolized by the Water Bearer, lives in the sky; Virgo is a creature of the earth. It's not just that these two signs have little, if anything, in common—they don't even live in the same world.

Aquarius finds meaning in the general principles of life. Virgo finds it in the details. Aquarius is a dreamer who wants to change the world; Virgo is a realist who wants to figure it out. Aquarius lives for the future, Virgo for the present.

These two signs share a reputation for eccentricity. Others often mistake Virgo for a picky control freak obsessed with details while Aquarius is viewed as an amiable oddball. These signs frequently see each other that way as well. The Virgin thinks Aquarius is unconventional, even fanatical, and Aquarius will say that Virgo is fussy and rigid.

Most of the time this pair is together will be spent arguing. Both love to talk and debate issues. Aquarius delights in tearing apart arguments by pointing out exceptions to Virgo's rules. For the Virgin, this is not only annoying but also a shattering denial of the very order Virgo so painstakingly constructed out of chaos.

Physically, this relationship may be frustrating. Neither sign is wildly passionate, and each will rely on the other partner to make the first move. This might result in long stretches between lovemaking, denying them both the physical intimacy they need but are unwilling to initiate.

A business relationship is not likely to prosper. Being a grand success is not an important goal for either; they just want to improve the world. The Water

Bearer and the Virgin could have the most efficient, well-run business in the world—if either of them had the motivation to seek out business or clients.

What these signs will offer each other is an engaging glimpse into a different world. But it will take a strong dose of fate to draw them together. For Aquarius, the world is somewhere beyond the galaxy; for Virgo, it is under a microscope. Fate, however, is bigger than the universe and smaller than a DNA molecule. If and when it strikes, it may leave these two perpetually puzzled.

## Virgo with Pisces

### *(February 20–March 20)*

Just when Virgo feels content that everything is proceeding according to the Virgin's viewpoint, along comes the Fish. Pisces, a water sign, is difficult for earth sign Virgo to grasp. Like water, shifting and unpredictable, Pisces is hard to contain. And what is true today about the Fish may not be true tomorrow. Pisces is ruled by intuition and feeling, not by pragmatism or reason. For analytical Virgo, this way of being can be particularly frustrating.

Because Virgo and Pisces are opposite signs in the zodiac, they both attract and repel each other. They must work to balance their opposite qualities or be constantly at odds. For the Fish and the Virgin, attraction is much stronger than resistance because both these signs are receptive or compliant rather than fixed or stubborn signs.

Pisces is a daydreamer, often only haphazardly involved in the most rudimentary details of life. Its home will be messy; it has little ambition or drive. But somehow the Fish manages to realize its most far-fetched fantasies. This incredible ability to make dreams come true arouses admiration and envy in the Virgin. It's difficult for practical Virgo to understand Pisces' success—especially since the Fish appears to be doing nothing to achieve it. The Fish simply dreams and the world seems to mold itself to its visions.

Surprisingly, the intuitive Pisces is strongly attracted to analytical Virgo. The Fish admires the Virgin's efficient, critical thinking, its ability to handle details, and its practical, orderly approach to life.

Still, the Fish tends to drift from relationship to relationship. These two signs may come together, but they can just as easily come apart. A business partnership will work if both will let it. Pisces

wants to succeed but needs direction. If Virgo will stay ahead of Pisces, it can keep the Fish on course. However, this won't be an easy task since elusive Pisces wants to swim in both directions at once or just drift with the tide. Virgo may quickly tire of Pisces' inability to stay the course on its own.

Friendship or a brief love affair will allow these two the most enjoyment of each other. The difference in their fundamental natures will not be a hindrance in the short run—in fact, that's the attraction. But for the long run, a lot of hard work will be necessary to bring the dreamy, escapist Pisces far enough down to earth to please the Virgin.

The text of this book was set in Bembo
and the display in Caslon Open Face
by Crane Typesetting Service, Inc.,
West Barnstable, Massachusetts.

Book design and illustrations by
JUDITH A. STAGNITTO